DewDrops On The Water Lillies

Anita Devi Powell

BookLeaf Publishing

India | USA | UK

Made with ❤ on the BookLeaf Publishing Platform
www.bookleafpub.in
www.bookleafpub.com

Dedication

This book is dedicated to sisters. Sisterhood and support have always gone hand in hand for me because of my amazing big sissy! The relationship we've grown into is so beautiful and sweet that whenever I need to cry, vent, try something new, or celebrate she is the first thought in my mind.

But she is not the only sister that I should highlight here, over the years I've always had a strong-willed woman in my life to fit my era and stand by my side, so shout out to all of these gorgeous ladies as well! Thank you so much for being in my life then and now, no matter how often we talk or see each other. You are all a very important part of my story and I wouldn't be here without you.

Preface

2025 is a year of growth and peace. We're all about healing our inner child, taking care of our own needs, and becoming the very best versions of ourselves. I really struggled with this book because I've been so burnt out in 2024 and simply couldn't find the inspiration to pull myself out of that dark hole of despair to flex my creativity. Somehow, in the new year I managed to find my spark and powered through this book to inspire, relate, and share my story with all of you. Thank you so much for supporting me and good luck on your journey to finding your inner Goddess!

Acknowledgements

I have to make a VERY special acknowledgement to my super supportive husband and kids! The past few years have been so hard to get through and no matter how overstimulated or overwhelmed I am, they show me so much love and kindness. From Anthony going out of his way to pick up the slack, to Maya being my sounding board, Joelle giving me all of the encouragement and confidence boosts, and Adonis being the perfect little baba and bringing me all of the candy and snacks while I'm lost in the zone. I'm so lucky to have such a phenomenal family that stands by me as I chase my dreams.

And For You, My Lovely...

To the women who bloom with grace,
Like flowers that rise from the earth's embrace,
With strength in their roots, and fire in their soul,
You are the goddesses who make us whole.

To the mothers, the sisters, the daughters who rise,
Like petals unfolding beneath endless skies,
With courage like thorns, yet tenderness, too,
This book is for all of you.

May you always bloom, even in the darkest of days,
A reminder that strength can appear many ways.
With faith in your heart and power in your hands,
You are the flowers who transform the lands.

Kali

She stands in shadows, fierce and free,
A goddess clothed in mystery,
Her hair a storm, her eyes aflame,
A force of life that cannot tame.

With every step, the earth does shake,
A wild dance for the world's sake,
She slays the demons, dark and vile,
Yet wears a grin, a knowing smile.

In her hands, the sword of truth,
A power born from ancient youth,
She crushes fear with every cry,
For in her rage, we learn to fly.

Her love is fierce, her touch divine,
In chaos, she draws a perfect line,
From death, she births the world anew,
A cycle vast, eternal, true.

Goddess Kali, fierce and wild,
You are the mother; I am the child.
In your grace, we are reborn,
From shadows deep, remove the thorn.

Lullaby

Swaying back and forth with you in my arms,
Effortlessly falling for your unspoken charms.
Once upon a dream lofting in the room,
I feel your love come into bloom.
Everything I wanted and hoped and prayed,
Now that I have you, I am never afraid.
My darling baby boy, so cuddly and sweet,
Never will the ground kiss your feet.
I will hold you close and near to my heart,
And I promise you we will never part.
You are my whole world, my moon and stars,
Whatever dreams you have, they now are ours.

Burn Book

Heart break and heart ache, were never expected.
Never opened my circle, never really connected.
I welcomed you in and gave you a place,
You took it for granted and spit in my face.
And now you try to repair the pain,
But I know for a fact you can't fix this sprain.
I trusted you with my family and thoughts,
But you turned out like the others, a sea full of bots.
I won't wish for your downfall or hope you crash,
Because I know everything you touch will turn to ash.
So please keep watching and lurking for clues,
Copycats don't get cheers... only boos.

The World Stands Still

Sunshine on my face and the earth at my feet,
Happiness and love make the air feel complete.
Tall trees swaying, their branches so free,
Heart songs chirping, soft as can be.
The scent of flowers, warm and sweet,
Whispers of peace, so calm and neat.
The world feels still, as if time's not there,
A moment pure, beyond compare.
The sky is a canvas, wide and bright,
Painted in hues of golden light.
My heart is open, wild and free,
At home, at last, in harmony.

Passion and Chaos

A flame consumes,
untouched by reason.
In the chaos,
we are both lost and found,
breath sharp, hearts wild—
the world tilts and spins,
and we dive deeper,
where nothing makes sense,
but everything feels true.
Our hearts beating in sync.
Time slows, a quiet space,
As the world fades, just me and you.
The warmth of you, so close, so near,
A perfect stillness, tender and soft.
In this moment, all feels right—
Just us, entwined, lost in our own dimension.

Bad Beti

Keeping everyone at arm's length, it's killing me softly,
The weight of their eyes, always watching, so lofty.
I want to breathe, to be myself without fear,
To live my truth, unapologetic, clear.

Log kya kahenge? They say with a frown,
But I *don't care*, I'm breaking it down.
These chains, these rules, they're holding me tight,
But I'm meant for more than this shadowed fight.

I want to laugh, to live, and be free,
To dance in the moment, just being me.
This world is short, and time slips away,
I won't waste it hiding, I'll chase the day.

The dreams inside me are far too bright,
But they're smothered by worry and endless fright.
I know I'm meant for more, to stand tall and true,
But first, I must break through these walls they
construe.

No more living in shadows, no more quiet plea—
I'm done with the fear, now I'll just *be*.
To be my best, I must rise and take flight,
Break free from the chains and embrace my own right.

Persephone's Pain

Beneath the earth, where shadows lie,
She fell through realms of empty sky,
A whisper soft, a hand so cold—
A kingdom dark, where souls are sold.

Her voice was silenced, once so bright,
Now echoing in the endless night.
She tends the flowers and touches grass,
Her demeanor changes, little sass.

In Hades' throne, she learned to grow,
A queen of pain, where shadows flow,
Yet in her heart, the light remained,
A flicker small, though deeply strained.

Her trauma forged her strength anew,
A goddess born from sorrow's dew,
She rose from grief, her crown of red,
A blooming soul from what was dead.

Language of Love

He covers my eyes as the sun rolls in on Sunday afternoon.

He meets me in bed with chai or coffee, 2 sugars 2 cream, just the way I like on a Monday Morning.

Coming home from work with red bull and chocolate in hand on a tired Tuesday evening.

Back rubs, head scratches, while laying in bed feeling his warmth on my frozen feet on a cold Wednesday night.

"But you always look beautiful" even though said on a Thursday, the words ring in my ears for days at a time.

"Come look at the moon" he calls through the house and holds me on a Friday night.

"Let's get caribou and go to the mall" are my favorite words uttered from his lips even though I know he wanted a lazy Saturday in.

These small items linger, so soft and true,
Reminding me of his love, in all he does too.

Blindian Babies

Collard greens and yams send my toes in a curl
Pani puri and doubles with slight heat that hurls
Juneteenth with the baked mac n cheese
Holi and Diwali with mithai sweet as a breeze

Gospel hymns and jazz that fills the air
Bollywood beats, rhythms everywhere
A Sunday sermon, the preacher's loud voice
Bhajans and kirtans, where spirits rejoice

Braids and beads, the art of the weave
Henna on hands, up arms like a sleeve
Mama's hands in the kitchen, love in the stew
Nana's hands weaving stories, old and true

Melanated and powerful, made with paint & with chalk
Sarees and turbans, pride in each walk
Harlem nights and fried chicken delight
Chai on the porch, under the moonlight

Both cultures rich, in spice and song,
Rooted in history, resilient and strong.
Different paths, but the same sacred earth,
Shared stories of struggle, joy, and rebirth.

This is what my children will grow and learn.
For love and flavor, they will never yearn,
From Nanie's kitchen to Granddaddy's yard
Words of affirmation and knees slightly scarred.

So are the ways of Blindian Babies,
Cultures mixed like a melting pot of maybes.
Will they feel caged or will they roam free?
I guess we will all have to wait and see.

Visions of Sugar Plums

Gold border and black and white,
Shades of pink to bring the light.
Mother Kali and impactful quotes,
Not the typical cars and boats.

We're setting high goals and doing big things,
I'm manifesting more than diamond rings.
I want to see the blessings unfold,
I want to share what remains untold.

The universe has plans for me,
I'm bringing nothing but main character energy.
My angel number and ins and outs,
Reminders to pray and water my sprouts.

No comparing to strangers so thin,
More authenticity, let it all in.
Be a nice human and keep the Nazar away,
Bring in big clients and get that payday.

Taking rest and more self-love,
Good energy being sent from above.
Rebranding into a badder bitch,
Passports and travel to scratch the itch.

Passion and romance, a love that burns bright,
Be soft with yourself, you can't do everything right.
So let the community say what they want,
And don't let those thoughts come in to haunt.

Breaking the cycles and plants so green,
A new vision has been seen.
2025 please be as good as you can,
Give me a big house with a VW Van.

Well Being

Within this group, I've found my place,
Breaking stigmas, a friend's embrace.
Building community, strong and true,
Filling the need for what we're due.

Mental health is a journey we now see,
A path to healing—mind, body, spirit, free.
Together we rise, together we mend,
A legacy of strength that will never end.

Through every conversation, every shared breath,
We conquer the silence, defy the depth.
In unity, we heal, we learn, we grow,
A light of hope in every heart we know.

Just a Little Crush

Shahrukh Khan's charm, so rare to find,
Rahul has me in a chokehold, I'm in a bind,
His smile like a star, so warm and bright,
The King of romance, in love's pure light.

Prince with his voice like velvet and gold,
A mystery wrapped in stories untold,
He dances in moonlight, so cool, so grand,
With every note, he takes my hand.

Little Zuzu with his fire and soul,
A warrior with a heart made whole,
His journey of redemption, fierce and true,
He found his peace, and I found him too.

Vegeta, proud with battle's might,
A warrior born for the endless fight,
Yet in his pride, a softness shows,
A complexity that endlessly grows.

Each one, a spark, a flame, a fire,
They set my heart to wild desire,
In worlds of wonder, they each play a part,
But these feelings can only live in my heart.

Little Bit of Self-Love

I'm healing my inner child,
With Furby's eyes that blink and smile,
Tamagotchi beeping for a while,
Snorlax, Gengar, and Pikachu,
Legos building dreams brand new,
Disney songs and castles bright,
Magic glimmering in the night.

I'm healing my inner child,
With tears that fall like gentle rain,
Hot cocoa with marshmallows ease the pain,
Stuffed animals to hold so tight,
Books that take me to new heights,
Uncle Iroh's calm, wise voice,
In every lesson, I rejoice.

I'm healing my inner child,
With a brand-new Nintendo and birthday cheer,
A cake that melts away all fear,
Dancing circles, spinning free,

Dress-up costumes, just to be,
Baby talk and giggles light,
Keepy uppy just feels so right.

Medusa's Power

Medusa's gaze, once soft and warm,
Now turned to stone, a shield from harm.
Her hair of serpents, twisting wild,
A symbol of a tortured child.
A beauty lost, a soul betrayed,
By gods who mocked the price she paid.
Her power grew from pain so deep,
A curse she wore, a wound to keep.

Once kind, once pure, she loved with heart,
But broken trust tore her apart.
The hands of those who sought her shame,
Left her with only fear and flame.
The earth trembled beneath her cry,
Her soul scarred beneath the sky.
And in her sorrow, strength did rise,
A fury born from endless lies.

I, too, have felt that bitter sting,
The weight of cruelty life did bring.

Like Medusa, trapped in pain,
I wore my scars and felt the strain.
But in the darkness, I found the light,
A will to stand, to claim my fight.
The world may judge and call me cold,
But in my heart, my power's bold.

I've learned that strength comes from the tear,
From every moment of despair.
Like Medusa, I rise again,
Not broken—healed, despite the rain.
My gaze may burn, my heart may weep,
But in my soul, the stones can't keep.
I wear my crown, no longer meek,
My strength, my voice—my truth I speak.

So let the world see what it may,
I, like Medusa, rise today.
My power forged in pain and fire,
A warrior born from all desire.

Chand Sitare

The moon, a goddess in the sky,
With eyes that shimmer, soft and sly.
Her light, a dance on waters wide,
Where tides obey and secrets hide.
She pulls at hearts with gentle might,
A mistress of both day and night.
In Hindu myth, her form divine,
Chandrama, where the stars align.

She whispers through the minds of women,
Guiding emotions, tender, driven.
In her light, we laugh and weep,
A cosmic force, both calm and deep.
From Lakshmi's grace to Shiva's power,
She rules each emotional hour.
She moves the oceans, vast and wide,
The ebb and flow, the shifting tide.

A force unseen, yet deeply felt,
In every tear and joy that melts.

Her influence, both soft and stern,
A cycle that we all return.
Like Yuwei, the Moon's embrace,
Balances power with gentle grace.
In her pull, we bend, we sway,
She leads the night, she lights the way.

The moon, in all her quiet splendor,
A goddess with a heart so tender,
Yet powerful enough to command,
The waters, the hearts, the shifting sand.
Her beauty, both serene and wild,
Is the moon, and she is the child.
Of time, of change, of endless flow,
Her light is everything we know.

Ano The Alien

Ever so clumsy, she falls to the ground,
No one near to hear the sound.
She laughs so loud and snorts with glee
Thinking about an old memory.
She changes her hair like you change clothes
Still it remains healthy with length that flows.
She's book smart and creative, a boss babe on her own
People stare and she turns them to stone.
She writes and rhymes and paints and bakes
Runs errands and cleans, she does what it takes.
She dresses so bright, tongue sharp like a knife
A goofball, a goddess, a good little wife.
She's a firecracker, dancing everywhere
Aura is glowing, she flips her hair.
Ano the Alien, so tiny and cute
Coming down from her spaceship, flexing her root.

Happy

Soft blankets with cutesy designs,
Fancy mugs with handles that shine.

Squishy slime in my hands,
Watching my daughter play trumpet in band.

Brushing hair on her dolls,
Praying together, we'll never fall.

SRK in Bollywood movies,
Jamming in the car to music so groovy.

Cuddling up under the stars,
Knowing that you're never too far.

Complementing others, "beautiful eyes",
Caribou runs, coffee or chai.

Laughter shared in the quiet nights,
In simple moments, we find our light.

Healthy

So many stairs but so little time,
Cilantro rice, smothered in lime.

Shredding the chicken, tearing to pieces,
Marinating deep, getting into the creases.

Stretching my arms, legs, and back,
Knowing that all I need is a good 'crack'.

Drink water by gallons and cups,
Refill after refill, filling it up.

Vitamins for me, for health and for mood,
It's just as important as my healthy food.

I'm taking care of me this year,
Health is a priority, no more fear.

Thriving

We say it every year and hope that it's true,
This is the year! For me and for you!!

Then halfway through we realize we're wrong,
But we know we have to keep holding strong.

I pray it goes well, and wish for the best,
But I already know it's just like the rest.

We feel the vibes and set our goals,
But we're all just stumbling around like foals.

Life is getting hard year after year,
All we can do is laugh and shed a tear.

This time it's different, I can feel it in my heart,
It's about time we get to the good part.

Shanti, Shanti, Shanti

Water lily sweet on the water; floating
Rays of sunshine on my face; doting
A beautiful book of poems; quoting
Growth and healing self; devoting

Gentle ripples in the air; soothing
Whispers of wind, so soft, eluding
The weight of worries, slowly eroding
In nature's arms, my soul is unloading

Colors dance as the sky starts to gleam
A tranquil heart, like a peaceful dream
Time stands still, in this quiet stream
Where all is calm and life feels serene